Contents

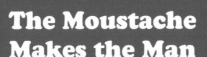

The Moustache Makes the Man

Never has there been a facial accessory as culturally charged as the moustache. To chart its journey through history is to chart the journey of masculinity itself, and to ask what makes a moustache is to ask what makes a man. It has been embraced with passion, and spurned with equal zeal.

Let us look briefly at its history. The moustache had its heyday between about 1850 and 1900 when it was a permanent fixture on the faces of all respectable gentlemen – a subtle indicator of breeding and gentility. Rudyard Kipling famously contended, "Victorian ladies would rather eat an egg without salt than kiss a man with no moustache".

However, as the 20th Century progressed, the fate of the mo in polite society became less certain. As western culture became more industrialised and comfortable, it repositioned itself on traditional interpretations of masculinity, and the moustache, as a result, slowly ebbed in popularity. In the 1940s and 50s, it became associated with foreigners, fools and fiends – Hitler, of course, had done it no favours, and Chaplin had infused it with comedic connotations. In addition, as the middle class grew, clean-shaven faces represented the move away from physical labour – a symbol of refinement and sophistication. For the working-class however, this was not the case, and the moustache quietly remained a mainstay of blue-collar workers, American figures of authority and military men.

In the late 1960s, the moustache experienced something of a revival amongst educated liberals, as *au naturel* hippie fashion brought back all types of facial hair. This was consolidated after the Stonewall Riots in 1969, when gay men began wearing moustaches along with flannel shirts, denim jackets and steel-toed boots – a proud statement laced with ironic reference to the figures of oppression and desire – working men and the authorities. By the 1980s, stoic stalwarts such as Hulk Hogan, Freddie Mercury and Tom Selleck stood strong, but the moustache had lost its way. It was simultaneously too gay and too straight – was it the mark of a hard, working man, or a camp inversion of male genitalia? This proved a semiotic conundrum too complex for most, and the moustache went underground for a full two decades.

So where does that leave the moustache today? Are they cool? Uncool? Or so painfully uncool that they're cool again? Laden with connotations, they are still treated with caution and yet, slowly but surely, they are inching their way back onto the top lips of stylish men. Men who have the prowess and confidence to recognise the erotic charge of the majestic moustache, regardless of sexuality.

A moustache is a delicate beast, and it's not for everyone. Like all style statements, a moustache is easier for some to carry off than others. Blonde mos easily side-step many of the Freddie Mercury/Groucho Marx/Anchorman/Borat references. But fair-haired men also lose out on the full impact of a truly bold moustache. For, unlike a beard, which carries with it an air of sincerity and prudence, the moustache requires its wearer to flaunt it with debonair casualness. There is nothing as tragic as an apologetic moustache, and as such it requires courage and character. It must be groomed and loved. Caressed and twirled. Worn proudly and with attitude. "I have a moustache and I am a man. Whatever that may mean."

Illustration by Stephen Kelly

INFLUENTIAL MOUSTACHES THROUGHOUT HISTORY	GROUCHO MARX	FRIEDRICH NIETZSCHE	ALBERT EINSTEIN	MAHATMA GANDHI

ADOLF HITLER	FREDDIE MERCURY	WILD BILL HICKOCK	SALVADOR DALI	JOSEF STALIN

FRANK ZAPPA	GEORGE ORWELL	DICK DASTARDLY	HOWARD HUGHES	MARK TWAIN

SADDAM HUSSEIN	WALT DISNEY	WILLIAM SHAKESPEARE	FU MANCHU	GEORGE CUSTER

Grow your Own

Growing a moustache is an exercise in patience. View it as a test of character, or a journey of self-discovery. Only those with true mettle will be able to last the distance.

Samuel Kenswil from Los Angeles.
Photograph by Zachary Ramey.

To grow a mo...

Don't shave. The pace of follicle growth varies from man to man, but the general rule is that it takes four to six weeks to grow a moustache.

★

Start growing it over a long weekend or a holiday so that you can introduce a more presentable moustache to the world.

★

After two or three days' growth, take stock, checking for bare patches, hair thickness and direction of growth, and then start thinking about a general style to aim for.

★

Try to ignore references to porn stars and the inevitable stupid questions such as "are you trying to grow a moustache?"

★

Around the second week it will start to feel very itchy as the hairs begin to curl under. Stay strong and use moisturiser.

★

In the early days your moustache might be a little unruly, but it should calm down as the hairs get longer and start to straighten out. At this point start combing it from the centre out to the sides, training the hair in a direction of growth.

★

Resist the urge to shape the moustache until it has reached maturity at four weeks. The hairs grow at different paces, so you have to wait and see what nature has given you before imposing your artistic vision.

★

There is very little you can do to speed up hair growth. Massaging the area may be of some use, and it is essential to get enough sleep and avoid stress. Some people believe that eating beef and/or drinking milk can aid follicle growth. Other supplements that may be of use are: biotin, vitamin A, vitamins B3, B6 and B12, vitamin C and vitamin E.

Giacomo from Parma.
Photograph by Richard Baker.

In a deck of cards the king of hearts is the only king without a moustache.

lugh from London.
Photograph by Richard Baker.

Peter the Great of Russia imposed a tax on men who wore beards, but not moustaches.

Which moustache is right for you?

You're growing a moustache! Good call –
but which one is right for you?

Firstly, work out how well your facial hair grows,
and where. Some men struggle to generate substantial
growth on their top lip. It might be a good idea to grow
a beard with the moustache at first, and then base your
design around the overall growth. Then follow these
simple rules:

Heavy face: a heavy moustache.

★

Long, narrow face: a thinner pencil moustache,
or a well shaped imperial-style tash.

★

Big nose: a medium or heavier moustache
to balance it out.

★

Big mouth/big teeth: a pyramid-shaped moustache
or handlebar.

★

Round face: a wide, rectangular moustache.

★

Square face: a long curved moustache
to soften the lines.

★

Pointy or recessive chin: a moustache-beard combo.

If in doubt take a black and white picture of yourself and
draw different styles of moustache on top.

nish Patel from Los Angeles.
hotograph by Zachary Ramey.

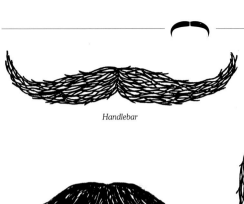

Handlebar

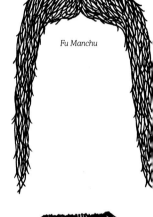

Fu Manchu

Pyramidal

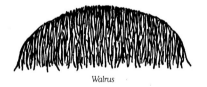

Walrus

Lampshade

Imperial

Chevron

Painter's Brush

Dalí

Horseshoe

Toothbrush

English

Adam from Chicago.
Photograph by Dave Mead.

The scientific term for the cultivation
of facial hair is pogonotrophy.

Researchers at Tel Aviv University have
shown that men with thin moustaches have
a greater propensity to suffer from ulcers.

Some tips

You might want to consider visiting a professional barber for the initial shaping of the beard. Once the contour has been defined, it is easy to keep it neat.

★

Invest in a wall-mounted mirror with a telescoping arm, so you don't have to lean across the bathroom sink to get a clear view.

★

Avoid high contrast, sticky foods – cream cheese for example. Always carry a handkerchief.

★

Your moustache will inevitably capture droplets of liquid when you drink. If this bothers you, you might want to carry a moustache cup, which has a special lip on the inside to space the hair from the fluid.

★

Tinted wax can help with GMS
(Ginger/Grey Moustache Syndrome).

★

You will have occasional 'bad mo days' just like you have 'bad hair days'. Groom as usual and try to get on with your life. Tomorrow will bring better mo.

★

If a girlfriend ever requests you remove your moustache, remove your girlfriend.

Ugo from London.
Photograph by Richard Baker.

In 1936, researchers found that if you attach a false moustache to the face of a wild female woodpecker, a male woodpecker will attack her as if she were a rival male.

According to the American Mustache Institute,
moustache approval ratings are between 16
and 35% in the USA, as opposed to Germany,
where they are between 72 and 94%.

Taking Care of your Moustache

An unkempt moustache is like having dirty fingernails or bad breath. Steer clear of the vagrant look, but also make sure you don't overgroom. A too-neat moustache can bring Major Dad to mind.

Bryan from Puyallup, Washington.
Photograph by Dustin Garrett.

Trimming

Wash your mo with a mild shampoo. Use conditioner regularly – this will keep the hair soft and silky. Make sure to rinse properly or the skin will dry out and go flaky.

★

Pat your moustache gently dry. Generally speaking blow-drying is not advisable.

★

Now for the trimming. It is important to prepare properly. If you are using scissors, make sure they are sharp tipped, however, many prefer commercial trimmers. Remember there will be lots of little hairs shed all over the place, so it is advisable to work in an easily cleanable area (think bathroom).

★

Shave just outside the line of your moustache, then tidy it up using the edging blade of the razor.

★

Using a moustache comb, comb against the grain of the moustache hair, so that it's standing up straight. Use a scissor over comb or clipper over comb technique to achieve uniform length and to remove bulkiness. Work from side to side. Bear in mind that wet hair is longer, so be careful not to cut too short.

★

Now comb the moustache so that the hair is going in the same direction, and check the length of the moustache for evenness at both corners of the mouth. Clean the edges with a trimmer.

Byron 'Bongo' from Hollywood.
Photograph by Richard Baker

The ancient Egyptians associated
facial hair with the sexual, religious
and social power of the monarch.

Ben 'Derben' from Berlin.
Photograph by Richard Baker.

The Amish believe that the moustache is an indicator of aggressive masculinity and therefore wear beards without moustaches.

Shaping

Depending on the style, you may wish to use wax or a wax/hairspray combination to maintain definition. Petroleum-based waxes can be difficult to wash out. Dishwashing soap can be effective in such an instance.

★

In the event that the hair is not co-operative, use a hair dryer to melt the wax, and hold the tip of the moustache in the desired position while the wax cools and hardens.

★

For just a few flyaway whiskers, a pomade will do. Beeswax lipbalm has also been proved effective for basic shape maintenance.

★

If not applying wax, use a moisturiser to soften the texture and keep your skin hydrated.

★

Always remember: groom what you have – not what you think you have.

★

Once complete, don a suit and look at yourself in a full-length mirror. Proper attire is of the essence when admiring one's handiwork.

Sean from New York.
Photograph by Richard Baker.

Charlie Chaplin's moustache was not real.
He described it as a prop "amusing enough to
add something to the routine, but that allows
me to keep my facial expressions".

Mark from Buxton, Derbyshire.
Photograph by Richard Baker.

All dolphins are born with a moustache.
It helps them locate their mothers while
nursing, and is shed after a few days.

Jay from St. Louis.
Photograph by Jay Morthland.

Get serious

The World Beard and Moustache Championships
recognises six official styles. All except the Natural
accept the use of aids – waxes, hairspray and
styling products.

Natural: a moustache styled without the
help of aids.

★

English: a slim moustache starting from the middle
of the upper lip with the hairs grown extremely long
and pulled to the side. Aids are allowed.

★

Dalí: a long, slender moustache with the tips
pointing straight out or arching up. Aids are allowed.

★

Imperial Moustache: a small, bushy moustache
grown until the end of the upper lip with the tips
arching up.

★

Hungarian: a big and bushy moustache, with the
hair growth stretching 1.5cm beyond the end of the
upper lip and the tips pulled to the side.

★

Freestyle: all moustaches that do not fit in the
other classes.

What do you call your moustache?

'Tache
'Stache
Mo
Moz
Muzzy
Mouser
Pushbroom
Soupstrainer
Face fungus
Nose bug
Lip spinach
Womb broom
Flavour saver
Momma's little helper
Mouth brow
Mr tickles
Cookieduster
Grassgrin
Prison pussy
Snot mop
Nose neighbor
The double hamster

BJ Monger from Santa Fe.
Courtesy of themonkeytail.com.

On average, a man with a
moustache touches it 760 times
in a 24-hour day.

Clockwise from right: Snyders from San Francisco. Photographs by David Gallagher. Butterscotch from Portland. Photograph by Pete Harrison. Felix from Quebec. Photograph by Vincent Roth.

The Moustache in Design

Now that the moustache is officially out of the doghouse, the simple beauty of its shape is finding its way onto everything from t-shirts to teacups, usurping even the swallow as icon of the hipster generation. These are a few of the best.

Mr Moustache tote bag
By Sirena con Jersey
www.sirenaconjersey.com

Moustache necklace
By Tatty Devine
www.tattydevine.com

Moustache handkerchiefs

By Avril Loreti

www.etsy.com/shop/avrilloreti

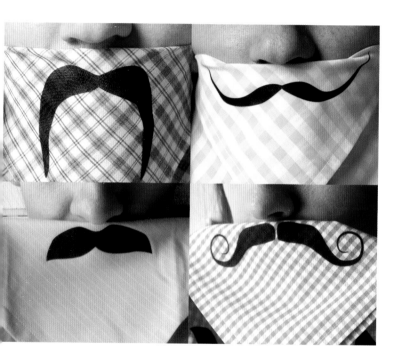

Salt and pepper shakers
By Jennifer Mortenson
www.etsy.com/shop/paperdollwoodshop

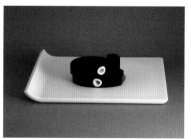

Mr Moustache baby mobile

By Jäll & Tofta

www.jaellundtofta.de

Incognito silver ring
By Melanie Favreau
www.supermarkethq.com/product/incognito

Moustache mugs

By Peter Ibruegger
www.peteribruegger.com

Moustache light
By Studio Greiling
www.katringreiling.com

Dog toy
By Humunga Stache
www.muttropolis.com

Moustache Typography
By Amaia Arrazola

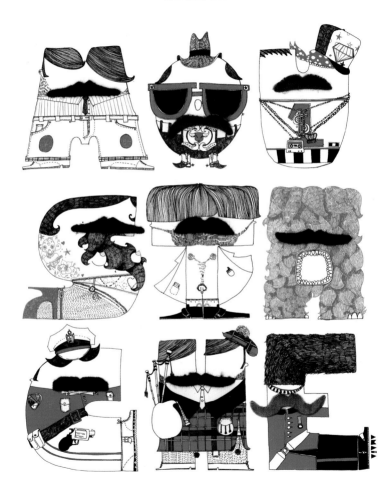

Pop's 'Stache
By Flatlab Design
www.flatlabdesign.com

Typographic Tash

By Katie Anderson

Stencil

Baskerville

Comic Sans

Helvetica

Futura

Chalkboard

Cochin

Impact

Aubury

Fake your Own

If for gender or follicular reasons you are unable to grow your own, these are some ways in which you too can sport a mighty mo.

Knitted Moustache and Beard

By Oyunga

www.ongidesign.co.uk

Materials

- two 50g balls of 4-ply wool,
  such as Rowan pure wool 4-ply
- knitting needles
- yarn needle
- polyester toy stuffing
- 60cm of clear elastic cord

What to do

1. Knit a rectangular strip approx
   12cm x 4cm (fig a). This will
   be your moustache.
2. Knit a triangular shape, approx
   12cm across, 5cm high (fig b).
3. Cut lots of short strands of
   wool about 4cm in length and
   knot these onto the triangle
   shape. It can be quite time
   consuming, but you will see
   your beard beginning to take
   shape (fig c).
4. To make the moustache, fold
   the rectangular strip in half
   and stitch across, leaving an
   opening in the middle.
5. Turn the strip inside out and
   stuff with polyester toy stuffing.
   Sew the opening shut (fig d).
6. Now sew down the middle
   of the tube shape that you've
   made to create a moustache
   shape (fig e).
7. Sew the moustache and beard
   parts together.
8. Measure out a length of elastic
   cord that fits around your
   head from ear to ear, and
   attach this to the moustache
   (fig f). Get hairy!

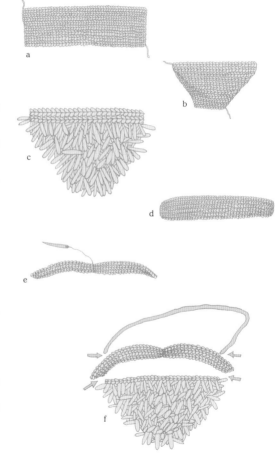

Crochet Handlebar Moustache

By Jessica Polka
www.jpolka.etsy.com

Materials

size G crochet hook (4.25mm)
worsted weight yarn
yarn needle

Skills

chain
slip
single crochet
increase
decrease
double crochet

What to do

1. Leave a 30cm tail of yarn when you make the first chain stitch; this will eventually be used to sew the moustache together.

   Row 1: Make a chain of 10 stitches, then slip in the first stitch you made, giving you a loop. (10 stitches in this row)

   Row 2: Double crochet in the first three stitches, single crochet in two, then slip in the last three, then single crochet in two. The purpose of these manipulations is to make the work bend. (10)

   Row 3: Repeat instructions for row 2. (10)

   Row 4: Repeat instructions for row 2, EXCEPT continue to slip for the last two stitches, rather than single crochet. (10)

   Row 5: Slip in the first three stitches. Single crochet in the next two stitches, double crochet in three, and then single crochet in the remaining two stitches. (10)

   Row 6: Repeat instructions for row 5. (10)

   Row 7: Slip in the first three stitches. Now decrease over the next two stitches, turning them into one. Double crochet in the next three, and then decrease again over the remaining two stitches. (8)

   Row 8: Slip in the first three stitches. Decrease over the next two stitches, turning them into one. Double crochet in the next three stitches. (7)

   Row 9: Single crochet in the first stitch. Then decrease over the next two, turning them into one. Single crochet in the next stitch, then decrease again, and finally single crochet in the last stitch. (5)

   Row 10: Decrease over the next two stitches. Single crochet in the next two stitches. (4)

   Row 11: Decrease over the next two stitches. Then single crochet in the last stitch, cut the yarn and tie it off. Work the end of the yarn back into the fabric so you can't see it anymore.

2. You now have one half of the moustache! Now repeat the instructions to make the other, and sew them together with a yarn needle, first row to first row, to form the shape shown. Instructions for adding loops or ribbons and for the other two mustaches can be found at *www.jpolka.etsy.com*.

Moustache on a Stick

By Stacy Scherf Dieterlen
www.oliveloafdesign.com

Materials

– celluclay (or if you're super
  crafty you can make your own
  paper mache pulp)
– small bowl of water
– 12 x 3/16" wooden dowels
– all purpose glue
– super fine sand paper
– acrylic primer paint
– acrylic paint in black, brown –
  or whatever colour you like
– varnish or Mod Podge

What to do

1. Follow the package instructions
   on the celluclay to make a small
   batch of paper mache clay
   (or make your own from
   scratch). Form the clay to your
   desired moustache shape – see
   pp. 14-15 for inspiration.

2. Continue to form and shape,
   smoothing out lines and
   crevices with a little bit of
   water on your finger or the
   end of a paintbrush. The more
   you smooth now, the less
   sandpapering will need to be
   done when the 'stache is dry.

3. Carefully insert the dowel into
   the left side of the moustache
   (or right side if you are left-
   handed!)

4. Allow to dry. This could take
   a few days. If you want to
   expedite the drying time and
   you have a small toaster/
   convection oven, put the
   oven on "bake" at the lowest
   temperature. Place your
   moustache on the oven rack,
   stick outside of the oven, door
   open. Heat at 10-15 minute
   intervals, allowing cool time
   in-between, until the piece is
   dry. Make sure you keep a close
   eye on it at all times!

5. Sand until smooth. Sometimes
   the stick can loosen from the
   moustache during the drying
   process – use an all-purpose
   glue to secure the dowel in
   the hole.

6. Apply a couple coats of Gesso
   or other acrylic primer, then a
   couple coats of paint in your
   colour of choice, and finally
   a couple coats of varnish or
   Mod Podge. Allow each coat
   to dry before applying the
   next. Et voila!

Photocopy this page and cut
along the dashed lines to create
your own moustache template
for printing.

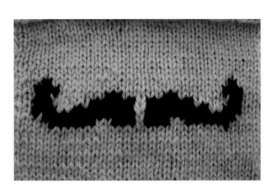

This moustache knitting pattern can be included into any knitting project using an intarsia colourwork technique, described in most how-to knitting books and websites. *Emily B Miller, standardd.net.*

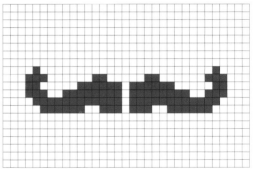

Ten more reasons to grow a moustache

You can raise money for charity. Movember
is a moustache-growing event held every November,
raising funds and awareness for men's health.

★

Women find men with moustaches irresistible. Similar
to a moose's antlers, it is inevitable that the man with
the biggest moustache will win the lady.

★

It enhances the enjoyment of alcoholic beverages,
allowing the wearer to savour individual drops in a
thoughtful and appreciative manner.

★

You can enter the World Beard and Moustache
Championships – the premier event in the field
of facial hair growth.

★

It will make you more manly.
Approximately 25% more manly.

★

No moustache is identical to another. The texture,
colour and shape of your moustache are proud
indicators of your bold individualism.

★

It adds more volume to your face and accentuates
facial features like eyes, cheekbones and jawlines.

★

A moustache lends gravitas and authority to even the
most pusillanimous of men.

★

It keeps your face warm in winter.

★

You can bond with other mustachioed men, secure in
your follicular superiority over the shaven masses.

Many thanks to all the photographers, illustrators, models and
designers who contributed material to this book. In particular,
Lee Roberts, Zachary Ramey, Jay Morthland, and especially
Richard Baker from bakerpictures.com, who was responsible
for a fantastic photoshoot in Hackney.

Published by Cicada Books Limited

Edited by Cigalle Hanaor
Designed by April, www.studio-april.com
Back cover illustration by Clare Owen

British Library Cataloguing-in-Publication Data
ISBN: 978-0-9562053-5-3

Printed in China.

Cicada Books Limited
76 Lissenden Mansions
Lissenden Gardens
London, NW5 1PR

T: +44 207 267 5208
E: ziggy@cicadabooks.co.uk
W: www.cicadabooks.co.uk